AF584108
South Australia
Victoria
Glenelg River
Port MacDonnell
Cape Northumberland
Flinty Point

Hi, my name is Ken Jones. I’m a proud Aboriginal Elder from Boandik Country in South Australia. I was born in 1951 in a place called Mount Gambier to a loving family. I had three older siblings and a younger brother. We lived on a small bush block near Port MacDonnell. I spent much of my childhood exploring this amazing area. My childhood adventures also planted the seed for my love of nature, and the importance of *Caring for Country*.

I can recall many happy memories of my times exploring and fishing. These memories often included my Dad, Bill. He taught me so much about the sea and the environment. Dad taught me how to sling a dragnet to catch fish at Pebble Point. He also taught me how to build eel traps and weave craypots so that they would withstand the forces of the ocean.

I remember going fishing with Dad when I was only four years old. Dad accidentally trod on my big toe. I cried noisily until he put three little tommy ruffs in a bucket to keep me amused. It worked and I stopped crying. I can still remember those three little fish swimming around in circles and looking up at me. I'm sure they wondered what all the fuss was about!

KJones

When I was a bit older, we used to go out fishing to a place called Flinty Point. This was home to some very big crayfish. Dad was once a commercial fisherman and he really knew how to catch them! We used to also catch freshwater crayfish in the creeks. We called them prickly backs. They were not very tasty compared to our Kela. This is the name we gave to our delicious saltwater crayfish.

HJones

During the winter months, we used to set woven eel traps in the freshwater creeks and billabongs. We gathered slimy, brown snails for bait and checked the traps each morning. We could catch up to a dozen big eels each day! We caged them at home in the cattle water trough. When we had about twenty eels, we would light up the charcoal fire pit and smoke them in the stone smokehouse.

This ancient tradition has been practised for thousands of years and is still continued by our family today. There were lots of smoke houses in the area. The Boandik People used to trade smoked eels for things like stone axes and bush medicines. Smoked eels are very well-preserved and they are still sought by many locals and visitors today.

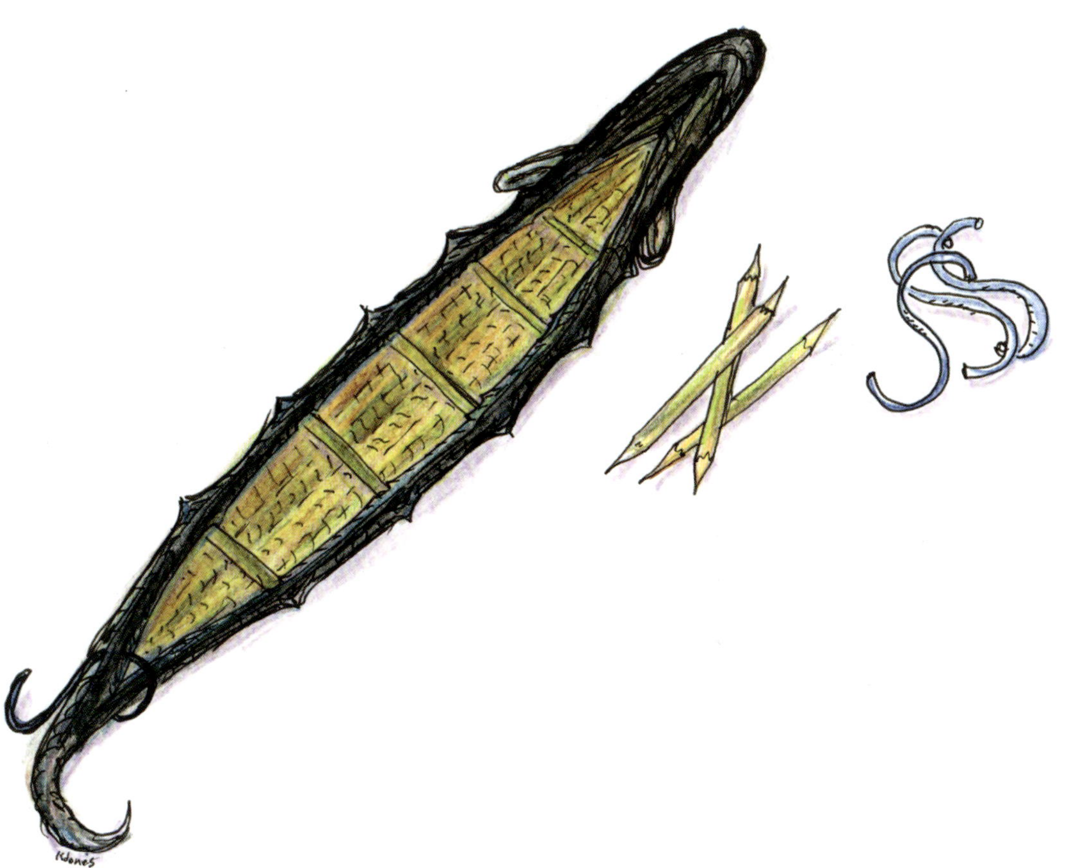

Dad told us a story of how he and old Bob Hammond used to trap freshwater rats near the creek. They used to drop hot mutton fat on to the steel traps and set them by the water's edge. When the rat crawled out of the creek, it would lick the fat until the trap went off. Snap! They used to skin the rats and sell the pelts to the local skin buyer.

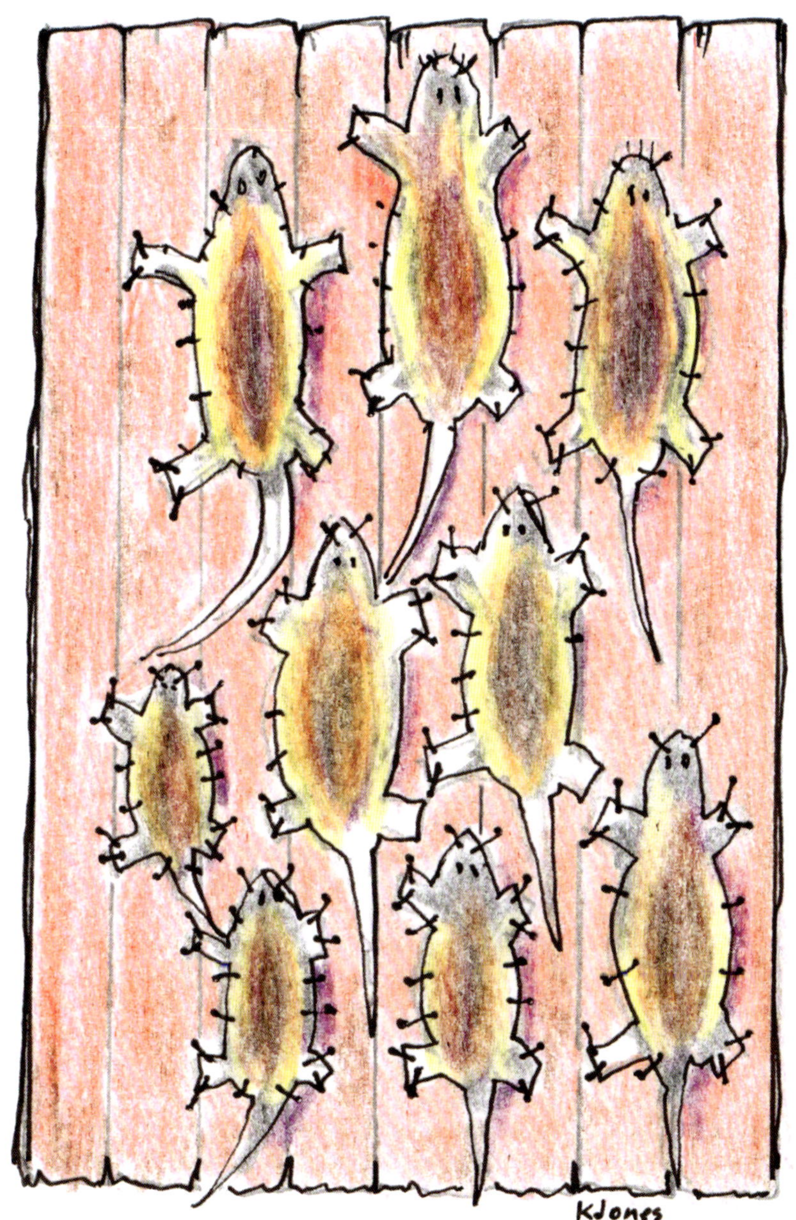
KJones

We used to also go duck shooting and rabbit trapping as well. Our lovable Labrador dogs would help retrieve the ducks for us. Mum was an amazing cook and would cook them up for us on the wood stove. We used to trade the rabbit pelts for cartridges and cash, so that we could do more shooting. I remember one time when we had problems with the giant wedgetail eagles stealing our rabbit traps. Sometime later, Mum found all six missing traps at the base of their nest tree. The eagles had taken the rabbits, traps and all, back home to feed their baby chicks!

KJones

One rainy day, we found two orphaned ringtail possums. They had lost their home in a storm. We cuddled them all the way back home and begged Mum to help us bottle feed them. We fed them fruit and nuts and gave them lots of love and care. They even slept with us in our old wooden sleep-out bunks! They lived with us for many months until we released them back into the wild to be real possums again.

Ringtail possum

I used to go beachcombing on the shores, especially when it was rough. It wasn't safe to go to sea at these times. Near Flinty Point, we found drift bottles from many foreign shores. We also found buoys, trawl nets, sisal rope, glass floats, and even shipwrecks. I also used to explore the caves near the shore. I even got stuck upside down in Kerr's Cave once!

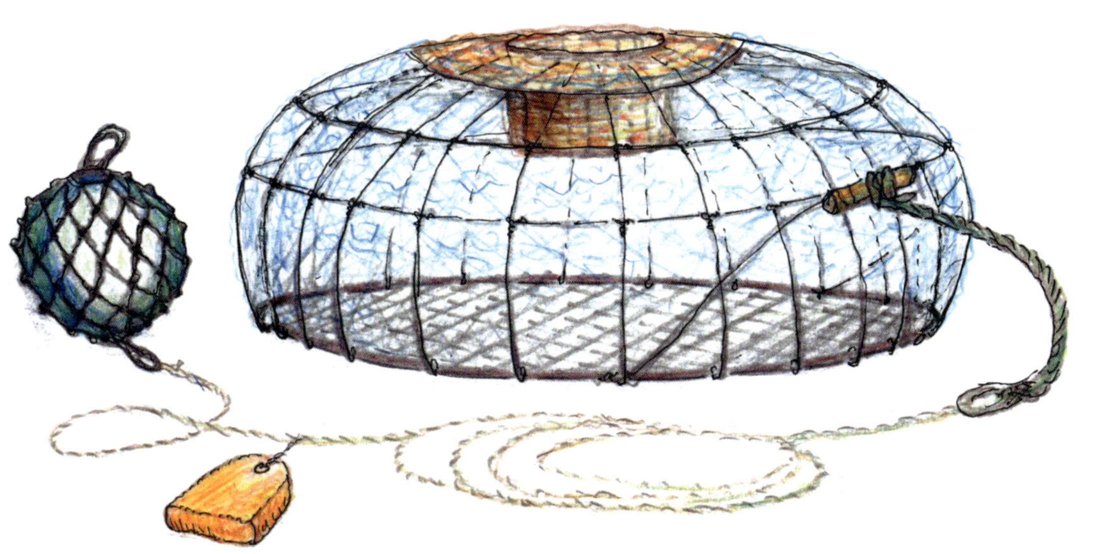

You could find all sorts of wildlife on the shoreline after a storm. There were angry elephant and leopard seals. There were sea lions and stranded whales, and sharks. We often found mutton-birds and penguins. We even found giant wandering albatross, and giant petrels with leg bands from South Georgia. There was always plenty of driftwood to carve with after a storm, like this carving of a banjo fiddler ray. The shoreline was a kaleidoscope of flotsam and jetsam. I loved my childhood by the sea!

Word bank

Aboriginal
Boandik
Australia
Mount Gambier
siblings
Port MacDonnell
adventures
importance
exploring
environment
dragnet
withstand
accidentally
noisily
wondered
Flinty Point
commercial
fisherman
freshwater
prickly

delicious
billabongs
gathered
dozen
smokehouse
ancient
tradition
continued
medicines
preserved
sought
visitors
Labrador
retrieve
cartridges
wedgetail
orphaned
ringtail possums
beachcombing
especially

foreign
buoys
sisal
Kerr's Cave
elephant
leopard
penguins
albatross
petrels
South Georgia
driftwood
banjo fiddler ray
kaleidoscope
flotsam
jetsam